DNA: *at the core of life itself*

By LAWRENCE LESSING

and the Editors of FORTUNE

Illustrated by MAX GSCHWIND

THE MACMILLAN COMPANY, *New York*

COLLIER-MACMILLAN LTD., *London*

*The author wishes to acknowledge with special grati-
tude the assistance of Miss Betty Fullen of Fortune's
research staff in the preparation of this book.*

*The contents of this book first
appeared in the pages of Fortune.*

Library of Congress Catalog Card Number: 67-22155

First Printing

The Macmillan Company, New York
Collier-Macmillan Canada Ltd., Toronto, Ontario
Printed in the United States of America

DNA: *at the core of life itself*

Contents

List of Illustrations

DNA: *at the core of life itself*

1 *The Master Key to Life*

Within the next few years, man is likely to take the first epic steps toward modifying directly his own hereditary structure. The first application of this new power will probably be an attempt to correct certain genetic faults leading to such disorders as hemophilia and muscular dystrophy. But, at the same time, scientists may well be prepared to intervene in such normal hereditary traits as hair and skin color, body build, and even in such less tangible areas as brain function and mental ability. Some authorities think most of this will come about in an experimental degree within the next five years, others that it will take much longer. But nearly all responsible

Strand 1

Strand 2

The master genetic key to life is this most renowned of all chemical molecules—deoxyribonucleic acid or DNA. Its unique double-stranded, spiral-staircase structure was first postulated in 1953, after a long and arduous search. DNA is located in the chromosomes of each living cell, and through a coded sequence of chemical units in its inner structure it directs the reproduction and development of every living organism on earth.

The two major strands of the DNA helix are composed of sugar-phosphate units endlessly repeated. These form the outer, acidic part of the molecule, and are everywhere the same in all DNA's. The stairs of the spiral are formed by four types of "base" compounds, attached to each strand at precise intervals and joined in the center by hydrogen bonds. The four base units are complementary—i.e., base A (adenine) will fit or join chemically only with T (thymine), and G (guanine) only with C (cytosine). The order in

2

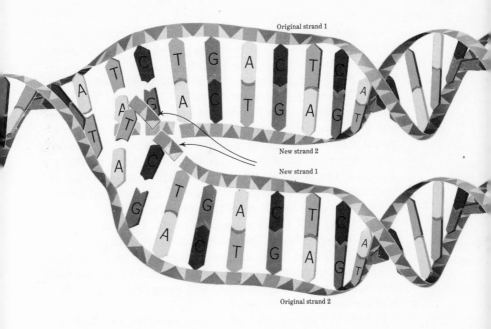

New strand 2

New strand 1

Original strand 2

which the bases occur along the strands varies widely, and it is this variable sequence that makes up the genetic code.

The first important function of DNA is to reproduce itself in cell division, so that each daughter cell gets an exact copy of the genetic code contained in the parent. The molecule shown above is in the process of reproduction, unzipping itself down the middle, as its base units break apart at the hydrogen bonds. Two exact replicas of the original molecule then form on the two separated strands as new complementary base-and-strand units are assembled from surrounding matter in the cell. Thus the code is transmitted from cell to cell and, by parental recombination, from generation to generation. The second important function of DNA is to apply the code to the shaping of protein molecules that make up the body of cells and of whole organisms. This is described on page 8.

3

scientists are agreed that the revolution known as molecular biology is just about to burst out of the laboratories, with incalculable effects on human life.

For well over a decade this biological revolution has been rolling up in successive waves of discovery. The first great wave came with the revelation in 1953 that the central and controlling germ plasm in all living things is contained in a giant, double-stranded, spiral-shaped molecule—the now famous deoxyribonucleic acid or DNA molecule. The study of this vital structure showed that it contained, in the variable sequence of its chemical units, an intricate code that directs the reproduction and growth of each living cell and organism on earth. The code directs growth by specifying the composition and shape of the thousands of protein molecules forming the major structures and regulatory mechanisms of life. The key to the code has now been uncovered, and researchers are busy working out its myriad practical details.

The second big wave of discovery, overlapping the first, rose about 1960, when biologists got the first glimpse of the complex system by which DNA controls not only the form and function of a single cell, but also the orderly development of many different cells making up a complex organism such as man. The search for the key to this master regulatory system, which controls the organization (and disorganization) of cells, is now also being hotly pressed in many laboratories. Meanwhile, a third wave of discovery is just rising, based on the first tenuous links that have been found between the genetic substance and the functioning of the nervous system and the brain, mainly in such areas as memory and learning.

In the pages that follow we will consider these three major phases of the biological revolution, and their profound implications for medical science and the future of man. The new knowledge is likely to put in the hands of men immense powers—for good or evil—comparable to those let loose by knowledge of nuclear energy. For the ability to change human life at its genetic source is the power, at its ultimate, to control the character of populations and to change the course of civilization in ways unparalleled in the past. It may well be the most fateful development thus far in all the ages of man.

A century ago, in 1866, the Abbé Gregor Mendel of Austria laid the foundations of classic genetics with his famed observations on the crossbreeding of pea plants in his monastery garden. Mendel's great insight was that traits are passed on from parents to offspring, with almost mathematical regularity, in small unseen units or packets. By observing how such traits as seed color or texture are transmitted from generation to generation, he formulated some of the basic laws governing the combination and recombination of his unseen units. In the early 1900's the American biologists Walter Sutton and Thomas H. Morgan theoretically located these packets, called genes, in the living cell on long, microscopic, rodlike bodies called chromosomes, which were seen to pair and divide in much the same way that Mendel had postulated for his invisible units. In 1927, Hermann J. Muller and L. J. Stadler of the U.S. independently showed, by irradiating fruit flies and corn, how changes or mutations could occur in individual genes, strung along the chromosomes, to account for varied traits within species and the evolution of species.

By the early part of this century, enough had been learned to set the framework of genetics and to influence powerfully the course of plant and animal breeding. Indeed, most of the great agricultural revolution of our time is based on these discoveries. But this genetics was almost entirely limited to the lower forms of life, to the manipulation of the total package of genes through whole organisms. Almost nothing was known in detail about what the package itself contained. No one knew precisely how chromosomes were formed or how they worked, and the genes remained pure abstractions. Until recently, biology was thus largely limited to studying life from the outside, and inferring, often brilliantly but sketchily, its inner workings from its many gross outward manifestations.

Arrival at a unifying concept

Now, however, scientists have got within the molecules of life to show, from the inside as it were, their real nature. This momentous inward voyage, on the atomic and molecular plane, was mounted largely in the 1940's, when the sciences of biochemistry and biophysics came together with powerful new instruments to probe life's hidden structures, beginning with some of the larger proteins. By the Fifties the expedition had reached the very core of life, thrusting aside the long-veiled mysteries of the genetic material. Chromosomes were seen to be primarily long strands of DNA, and the genes simply coded sequences of chemicals strung out along their lengths. In one sense this discovery was simply an extension of Mendel's germinal vision. But in another and deeper sense it marked a revolutionary advance, for in the structure of the genetic material biologists found a unifying concept as powerful and prolific as that of the atom in physics. Already it is drawing together many of the chaotic facts of life and unfolding new powers to order and control them.

Many voids remain to be filled in the new knowledge. The unifying concept of a genetic code in DNA begins to explain, but does not go far to reduce, the inherent complexity of life. Progress has been so phenomenally rapid, however, that there is every reason to believe the major gaps will soon be filled. Since 1953 knowledge in this area has just about doubled every two years. Textbooks are out of date before the ink is dry. By 1966, seven of the last thirteen Nobel prizes in medicine and physiology had gone to the field of molecular biology. Nearly all the major universities of the Western world are now involved in extending and settling this new frontier. (The Russians still lag because they were so late in giving up Lysenko's false doctrine that externally acquired traits are inheritable.) Already some of the big chemical and pharmaceutical complexes have sizable research teams at work trying to translate the new knowledge into new and viable materials that act upon the genetic system. This could well be the next big stage of development in the chemical industry.

How harmless bacteria become virulent

The trail leading up to this explosion was a long one. It had been known for a century that chromosomes in cell nuclei were made up of nucleoproteins, a combination of nucleic acid and protein. Indeed, the nucleic acid DNA had been isolated as early as 1869. Much later a second and closely related type of nucleic acid was found in cells; it was called ribonucleic acid or RNA. But, since the function of these materials was totally unknown, they were thought to be only incidental to the more important protein, which seemed to be the most characteristic substance of life. Chemists tried long and futilely to find the genetic key in the protein portion of the chromosomes.

Their view was further clouded by the then rudimentary state of biochemistry. Chemists could break down and

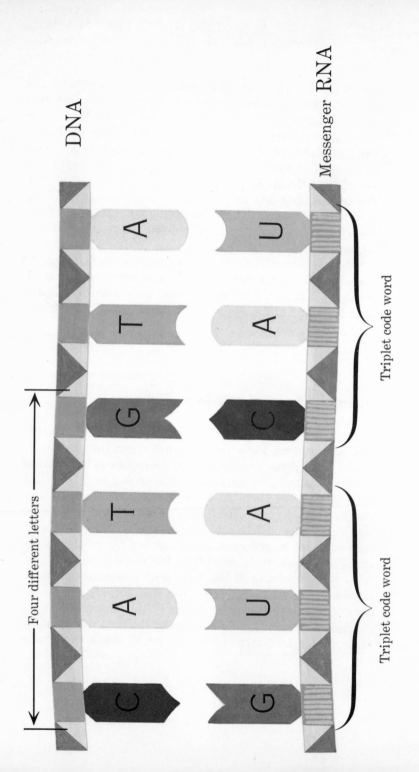

The language of life is cast in three-letter "words" from the coded sequence of four base compounds—A, T, G, and C—found in the structure of DNA. Each triplet is a code word that stands for one of the twenty or so amino acids that make up, in various orders and proportions, the great variety of proteins. At first it was hard to see how only four base "letters" could code some twenty amino acids; long experiments showed that the code letters had to be taken in three's. This diagram illustrates the beginning of the process of transcribing the code from DNA, cloistered in the cell's nucleus, and putting it in a form transportable to working sites in the cell. A short strip of DNA, which codes one sequence of amino acids for a protein, loosens its bonds, but instead of reproducing DNA it forms a complementary single strand of messenger RNA—a slightly different form of nucleic acid that carries DNA's instructions out into the cell. The strip of messenger RNA is now a "negative print" or exact replica of the triplet sequence in DNA. It drops off and finds its way into the cell fluid, where it is soon picked up by a roving particle of ribosomal RNA, another of DNA's intermediaries. The making of protein then begins, as shown on pages 10–12.

analyze such compounds as protein and DNA, but they had no idea how they were put together in the complex structures of life. Not until the late 1920's did chemists discover that major organic materials were built up from small, repetitive chemical units into giant molecules, whose complex architecture chiefly determined their properties. Out of this new concept flowed the plastics, fibers, and other synthetic wonders of the modern chemical industry. But the key molecules of life were much bigger and infinitely more complex than any of these.

The first clues to the structure and identity of these supermolecules were found in the most obscure and unlikely places. In 1928 an English bacteriologist named Frederick Griffith, trying to find out why certain bacteria

How a protein is manufactured

The end product of the genetic code in DNA is protein, the basic structural matter of life. In its endless variations on the twenty-amino-acid theme, protein forms flesh, bone, hair, eyes—all the color and motion of life. The process of building a protein begins, as seen on page 8, with DNA imprinting a portion of its code on a strip of messenger RNA. The strip is then picked up by a ribosome, a particle of ribosomal RNA floating in the cell, which acts as a protein factory. The messenger RNA is inserted in a slot in the ribosome, which then proceeds to "read off" the message word by word, like a punched-tape machine or tape recorder.

At each word in the message, designating a specific amino acid, a third type of RNA molecule moves in, called transfer RNA. It carries the particular amino acid called for, and proceeds to plug in momentarily to the base word in the messenger RNA tape. Each transfer RNA is so designed that it carries a specific amino acid at one end, and at the other a base unit that fits only the base word that designates that amino acid. Thus, one by one, following the exact order laid down in the DNA code, the proper amino acids are brought into line and welded into a chain that becomes a strand of protein, which may be anywhere from fifty to hundreds of amino-acid units long.

As the ribosome moves along the messenger RNA tape, making its protein, other ribosomes latch on to the disengaged end and start making their own strands of protein, on a kind of moving assembly line, as shown on page 12. For convenience, amino-acid "words" on the RNA tape are shown in numbers on page 12. In this process, first observed and worked out by Alexander Rich of M.I.T., thousands of complete protein chains are produced per minute from a single strip of messenger RNA. All together, some 100,000 different kinds of proteins are produced in the human body alone. The structure of each is specified by the DNA in the forty-six chromosomes found in man.

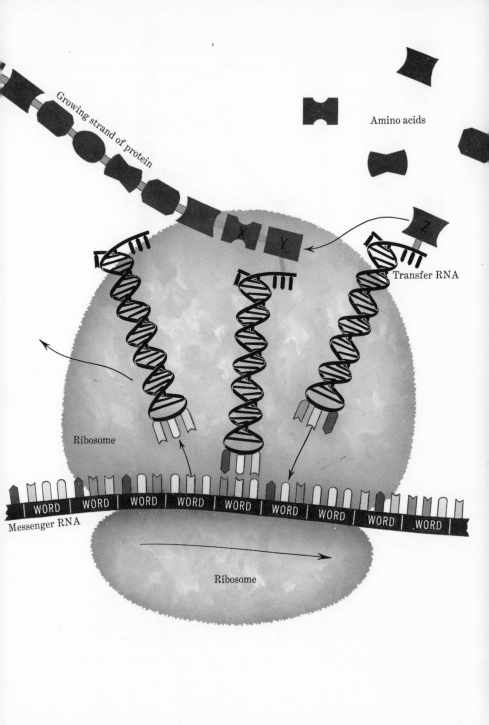

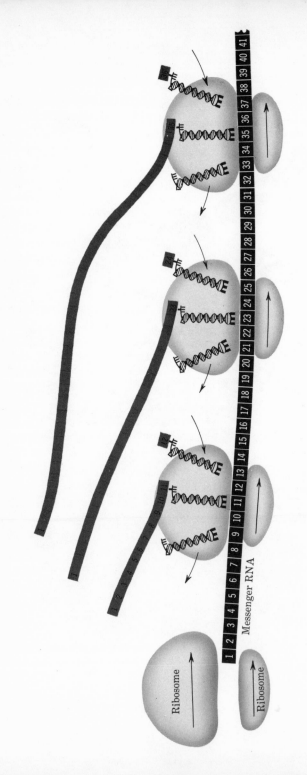

The ribosomal assembly line.

suddenly became virulent, reported an eye-opening experiment. He had mixed heat-killed pneumonia bacteria with live colonies of a benign type and found, by injecting the mixture into mice, that some of the harmless bacteria had been transformed into the virulent type. Later it was shown, in a test tube, that a mere chemical extract from the dead bacteria was sufficient to transform the harmless bacteria into the virulent. Moreover, the transformed bacteria passed on their new infectious character to all succeeding generations. In some way, never before encountered, the genes of one organism were being incorporated into the genetic material of another and different type of organism. A hunt therefore got under way to track down that portion of the chromosomes that was involved in the infective transfer, and perhaps there to discover, at long last, the nature of the telltale genes themselves.

In 1944, after years of painstaking labor, the prize of discovery went to a team at New York's Rockefeller Institute: Oswald T. Avery, Colin MacLeod, and Maclyn McCarty. They purified and repurified extracts from dead pneumococci and showed, in a dozen ingenious tests, that one and only one material in the chromosomes was the gene-carrying substance, and this was DNA. Stripped of all surrounding matter, the naked DNA alone had the power to transform one type of bacteria into another. In the lowly pneumococci the identity of the genetic substance was finally proved beyond all doubt, though its molecular structure still remained unknown. Subsequently, DNA was shown to be the hereditary material in viruses, other bacteria, and so on up to man.

A model in scrap tin

Nearly ten more years were required to bring the elaborate submicroscopic structure of DNA into view. This time it was a trio of scientists in England that brought off the coup. In a now famous "hut" on the grounds of Cambridge University, right after World War II, Francis H. C. Crick, a young Briton who shifted from wartime physics to the life sciences, and James D. Watson, an American biochemist, set out to find the shape and sequence of chemical units in pure DNA—in a sense, the shape of life itself. Simultaneously in King's College, London, Maurice H. F. Wilkins, an atomic physicist turned biologist, put x-ray diffraction techniques to work on crystals of DNA to get spectral pictures of the arrangement of their atoms. Working from Wilkins' clear pictures and their own chemical analyses, Watson and Crick slowly built a model in scrap tin of the molecule's main architectural features. They were aided by a suggestion made by Linus Pauling, the U.S. Nobel Prize winner in chemistry. Pauling had found that protein molecules were formed in the shape of giant spirals or helixes, and he suggested that the structure of DNA might be similar, since DNA must be intimately related to the formation of proteins. Watson's and Crick's great intuitive feat, however, was to deduce from still meager evidence that DNA did not have a single-stranded helix structure, as in proteins, but was a huge, entwined double helix—a structure that met all the requirements for a self-reproducing molecule. Eventually this insight, proved correct by a number of substantiating experiments, won Watson, Crick, and Wilkins the Nobel Prize in 1962. It was indeed a milestone, for only when the molecular structure of a substance is established can the substance be said to be truly known.

The structure of DNA that unfolded was a marvel of precision and beauty. The main strands forming the backbone of the double helix were composed of long spiral chains of sugar-phosphate units, endlessly repeated. These strands were joined together at regular unit intervals by small side chains, or "base" units, to form the well-known spiral-staircase structure of DNA. The base units, each attached at one side to a strand unit and joined in the center by a hydrogen bond, were generally composed of one of four related compounds: adenine (A), thymine (T), guanine (G), or cytosine (C). These bases were complementary—i.e., compound A would join chemically only with T, and G only with C. While the backbone structure of DNA was found to be uniform throughout nature, the order of the different base pairs varied along its double-stranded length, and varied even more widely from species to species. This variability soon led Watson and Crick to propose that the paired bases contained, in some way then unknown, a hidden code controlling all forms of life.

5,000,000,000 "bits" of DNA = man

The great DNA helix, alone of all the biological structures studied, had the size, configuration, and complexity required to code the manifold forms of life. It is, indeed, a unique and remarkable molecule. Concealed in its long, gelatinous strands, just visible in the electron microscope, is a structure tens of times larger than that of any other biological molecule. The number of paired bases alone, packed into the tightly twisted turns of the helix, ranges from about 5,000 for the simplest known virus up to an estimated five billion in the forty-six chromosomes of man. Biologists have tried in various ways to give laymen some idea of how much information such a structure can contain. One teaspoon of DNA from a variety of bacteria known as *Escherichia coli,* much used in genetic research, has an information capacity about equal to that of a modern computer with a volume of about 100 cubic miles. A single thread of human DNA, about five feet long, from a single cell contains information equivalent to some 600,-000 printed pages averaging 500 words each, or a library of about a thousand books.

The double and complementary nature of the DNA helix almost immediately suggested to biologists the method by which it reproduced itself in parthenogenesis and cell division. In 1957, U.S. Nobel Prize winner Arthur Kornberg showed in principle, by manipulating DNA in a test tube, that the DNA molecule simply unzips. Its two strands separate down the middle, breaking the hydrogen bonds. Then on the strands it proceeds to form, by the complementary attraction of new base units from surrounding cell matter, two exact replicas of the original double helix. In an elegant experiment on *E. coli* in 1958, Matthew Meselson and F. W. Stahl of the U.S. proved that this is, in fact, the way in which DNA replicates itself from cell to cell, almost with printing-press accuracy. But the method by which DNA blueprints the structure of the numerous other particles and processes within each cell was a much more complex and difficult matter to deal with. The essential problem was to see how only four base units in DNA could code or specify the exact order of structural units in proteins, which are long, complex, chain molecules made up of some twenty different kinds of amino acids.

This was a problem in cryptography that would have delighted Poe. A clue to the cipher came from theoretical physicist George Gamow. He used playing cards designating only the four traditional suits—hearts, spades, diamonds, and clubs—to illustrate the mathematical possibilities of translating a four-base code into the twenty elements of the amino-acid language. He showed that if three cards were drawn at a time, then the total number of possible suit combinations in the three-card hands was exactly twenty—that is, if the order of the suits within the hands was disregarded. The DNA code therefore was likely to be found in triplets—i.e., three base units taken together coded one amino acid. But the order of chemical units is important in biology, hence the order of bases within the triplets also had to be taken into account, and this promptly raised the number of possible triplet combinations to sixty-four—entirely too many to allow a simple code relationship of one triplet to each type of amino acid. Adding to the difficulties was the fact, soon discovered, that DNA did not directly form proteins but worked in a complex way through the secondary form of nucleic acid, RNA. For some years the whole coding problem remained confused.

The code is broken

In 1961, Crick performed an experiment that proved the triplet theory. By adding one base unit at a time to an RNA chain capable of synthesizing a protein, he showed that when only one or two units were added the RNA became inoperative, but when a third unit was attached it regained its ability to make protein. That same year Marshall W. Nirenberg and a group at the U.S. National Institutes of Health identified the first DNA code triplet with a specific amino acid. Using a technique devised by Severo Ochoa and a group at New York University, he built up short, synthetic chains of RNA out of a single type of base unit—representing an adenine triplet (AAA) in the DNA code—and showed that these chains produced a protein made up entirely of a single kind of amino acid, called phenylalanine. By introducing other base units into the synthetic RNA and observing their effects in protein synthesis, Nirenberg's and Ochoa's groups soon had related loosely nearly all of the sixty-four possible DNA triplets to the amino acids they code for. And Nirenberg went on to develop a new technique that has now positively identified all the triplets, and the order of their bases as well.

All this was doubly confirmed in 1965 by a team at the University of Wisconsin, led by H. Gobind Khorana, an Indian-born biochemist. Khorana developed a delicate technique for chemically synthesizing in a test tube short chains of DNA itself, with a known sequence of bases, and then following them up through all stages to the ultimate production of protein. Meanwhile in England a group at Cambridge University, led by Sydney Brenner, found one of the code's last, long-sought components. In another intricate experiment on *E. coli* bacteria, using chemicals to induce precise mutations in its DNA, they found that one particular code unit, heretofore thought to be a "nonsense" triplet coding no amino acid, appeared to act as a period or stop sign, signaling the end of one protein-chain synthesis.

The genetic code, in its main elements, is now broken. A sequence of triplets along the DNA strand denotes one complete amino-acid chain in a protein. In other words, the code consists of groups of three-letter "words" read off continuously along the strand, like a telegraphic or punched-tape message, but with no spacing between "words" until the message comes to a stop. Most of the words are redundant—i.e., two or more kinds of triplets stand for the same amino acid—probably nature's device to make sure the code works. What is even more amazing, the code appears to be almost universal: the same triplets code the same amino acids in all species. An ingenious experiment recently fused a strand of human DNA with a strand of mouse DNA in a hybrid cell; the result was the production of some proteins common to man and mouse. Thus the genetic code is the oldest of all languages, running back through evolution to the lowest bacteria, some of which, according to fossil traces found in 1965, appeared on earth at least two billion years ago.

How a gene transmits its instructions

The end product of the genetic code and of all genetic activity is protein. This, too, was first established in the germinal Forties, long before the genetic code was even conceived, by a series of Nobel Prize-winning experiments conducted at Stanford University by George W. Beadle and Edward L. Tatum. They worked, not on bacteria, but on the equally humble and now famous bread mold, *Neurospora crassa,* a fungus found capable of synthesizing all the amino acids needed for its growth from a simple chemical nutrient. By irradiation, Beadle and Tatum created mutant strains of the mold that were selectively unable to grow on the nutrient because, it was proved, they lacked one or another of the key proteins, called enzymes, that aided in the synthesis of a specific amino acid. Clearly, mutation had knocked out the gene controlling the formation of this key protein. This confirmed Beadle's theory formulated earlier that one gene equals one enzyme—i.e., one gene controls the formation of one enzyme.

Exactly how a gene transmits its instructions for the building of a specific protein remained a mystery, however, until about 1960, when a series of developments brought a clearer idea of the intricate role of RNA. This nucleic acid differs from DNA in only two important respects: it has one base unit different from DNA's, and it usually has a single-stranded structure. RNA had been found earlier in the cell, making up a large part of numerous, mysterious cell particles called ribosomes, which significantly seemed to be the sites of active protein synthesis. What was not perceived, however, was that there are other forms of RNA in the cell besides ribosomal RNA. In the mid-Fifties, M. B. Hoagland of Harvard Medical School discovered a second and smaller molecular form of RNA, which later was found to carry single, specific amino acids to the sites of protein production. This became known as transfer RNA. Then, about 1960, a number of U.S. laboratories almost simultaneously tracked down a third form of RNA; its existence had first been suggested by Jacques Monod and François Jacob of the Pasteur Institute in Paris, who recently became Nobel laureates. This third form, which turned out to be the key piece in the puzzle, was called messenger RNA, for it has the function of transcribing a strip of the master code from DNA and transporting it to the ribosomes. There it acts as a template or jig upon which transfer RNA's begin assembling amino acids to build a specific protein.

Many aspects of this mighty manufacturing process are still obscure. The exact functioning of ribosomal RNA is still unknown, beyond the fact that it seems to serve as a nonspecific, movable workbench on which any type of protein may be assembled. And the only kind of RNA whose structure is as yet fully known is transfer RNA; this was worked out only in 1965, down to the exact positions of its 2,500 or more atoms, by Robert W. Holley of Cornell University. Nevertheless, in this DNA-RNA-protein interplay we may now see the broad outlines of the intricate process by which life puts on individual tissue and integument, flesh and blood.

The traffic directors

The varieties of proteins are almost as infinite in number as stars in the sky. There is a large class of proteins called the keratins, which form skin, fingernails, hair, horns, feathers, scales, and the hard carapace of turtles. There are the collagens, which form bone, cartilage, tendons, and connective tissue. And the myosins, which make up the contractile fibers in muscles and the blood cells in mammals. All together, there are some 100,000 different kinds of proteins in man alone, each differing slightly from individual to individual, and each with a size and amino-acid sequence specified in the DNA code of the chromosomes.

But of all the proteins, the most numerous and vital by far are the enzymes, which act as catalytic agents in all biological processes. The function of a catalyst is to speed up chemical reactions without entering into them. Compared to many other proteins, enzymes are relatively small molecules, but of exquisitely specialized construction. Each type of enzyme is designed to activate only one kind or one stage of a specific biological reaction. One series of enzymes, for instance, breaks down the proteins in foodstuffs to make free amino acids available for cell growth. Other enzymes are active in the synthesis and construction, in prefabricated sections, of such huge proteins as blood hemoglobin. None of the larger structural proteins could, in fact, be built without enzymes. Even DNA is attended by its own enzymes, which aid it in reproducing itself and in synthesizing RNA. Enzymes, indeed, direct nearly all the traffic of life.

One entire branch of biochemistry has been hard at work elucidating the structure and workings of this crucial molecule. The enzyme's main feature is a highly wrinkled structure, with only two or three small active sites, which are shaped to fit exactly the molecular structure of the materials it works on, like interlocking pieces of a jigsaw puzzle. When two molecules that are to be joined approach the enzyme, its active sites momentarily lock into them, forcing them into such close proximity that they quickly link together. Alternatively, when a large molecule is to be broken apart, the enzyme strains its chemical bonds until they snap. A single enzyme can cleave or join thousands of molecules per second, faster than any known industrial catalyst. Biochemists now are not only pinpointing active sites in enzymes but building models of them with an eye to making active enzymes in the laboratory.

This intimate knowledge is being pursued not only for the light it casts on life's processes, but for the power it may provide to correct these processes when they go wrong. Enzymes are particularly vulnerable to damaging mutations or coding errors; a single change in one DNA base triplet that codes one amino acid in an active site is sufficient to block production of a workable enzyme. Indeed, most harmful mutations were first seen through their effects on enzymes. Albinos, for instance, are now known to lack the one enzyme needed to initiate synthesis of melanin, the protein pigment giving color to eyes, skin, and hair. The great hope is that such errors may be traced back through precise pathways to their genetic source and then corrected.

Many of the most mysterious and wasting of human disorders are now known to be caused by genetic mishaps. The first clear link between a molecular disorder and a genetic error was established in the late Forties by Linus Pauling and Harvey Itano, who showed that sickle-cell anemia, a disease prevalent in large regions of Africa, was traceable to a genetic fault that begot misshapen hemoglobin molecules. Even earlier, a genetic source was suspected as the cause of a disease leading to severe mental retardation in infants. The disease, since named phenylketonuria, was traced to the lack of an enzyme to break down phenylalanine, an amino acid in foods, causing toxins to pile up and poison the brain. Other disorders in which genetic errors are being implicated are galactosemia (lack of an enzyme to break down lactose in milk; this also damages the brain), agammaglobulinemia (lack of an enzyme forming gamma globulin in blood), and cystic fibrosis (lack of pancreatic enzymes for digesting foods). More are being discovered every year.

Genetic engineering

Up to now, the only way found to deal with these disorders has been by such peripheral measures as eliminating milk from diets. The new molecular knowledge opens two broad new lines of attack. The first of these is to synthesize specific enzymes or other biologically active materials, which may then be administered to the patient to make up for the body's deficiencies. This would be simply an extension of such well-established medical practices as supplying insulin to diabetics or estrogenic hormones to menopausal women. The second line of attack, and the more difficult one, because it has never been undertaken before, is to correct the body's errors at their source in the genes and chromosomes.

The first of these lines of attack is the most immediately promising. Techniques are well along for the synthesis of proteins, such as enzymes. Only in 1965 a new, automated method for rapidly synthesizing protein chains on plastic beads was announced by scientists at Rockefeller University (formerly the Rockefeller Institute). It may even be possible to simplify and improve on natural enzymes. Another intriguing idea is to synthesize or separate out other materials, further back in the genetic system, such as a specific messenger RNA, which may then be injected into the deficient cells to enable them temporarily to make their own missing enzyme. Recent work at Indiana University and the University of Edinburgh, Scotland, indicates this can be done. But all such techniques have one serious drawback: since they would be temporary in their effects, the patient would require lifelong treatment. Consequently, most of the research effort is now directed to the second, more revolutionary line of attack, to correct genetic defects at their source.

Only a year or two ago the task looked like a formidably·
long one. Sequestered in the cell nucleus, and more jealously
guarded than any other living molecule, the DNA in the
chromosomes is extremely difficult to get at. The major
problem is to find selective mutagens or carrier agents that
will get through the cell's defenses and replace a bit of its
DNA with a new, corrected base sequence. The first likely
agents to be explored were bacteria, in which the phenomenon of genetic transformation was originally discovered.
Carrying on Avery's work at Rockefeller, Rollin D. Hotchkiss
and his co-workers steadily refined the process, showing that
small purified fractions of DNA, containing only one gene
or a small group of related genes, could be effectively used
to insert specific new factors into bacterial DNA. Later, at
the University of Wisconsin, Elizabeth and Waclaw Szybalski
performed the same type of transformation on cultured
human cells, restoring to some the ability to produce a
particular enzyme. Bacteria, however, have serious draw-
backs as agents for carrying genetic corrections into the
human body, since they are not highly discriminating in
the types of cells they invade.

More promising agents are the viruses—the simplest form
of life, composed of only a single thread of DNA or RNA
with a protein coat—which are all highly specific in the
tissues they enter. In the more virulent types, the virus
literally injects into the cell its own DNA, which then proceeds to overwhelm the cell's genetic apparatus, forcing it
to produce more viruses until the cell is destroyed. Some
viruses, however, are relatively nonvirulent; they coexist or
lie dormant in cells, often attaching themselves to or becoming part of the cell's chromosomes. A decade following
the discovery of transformation in bacteria, Joshua Lederberg, who shared the Nobel Prize with Beadle and Tatum
in 1958, discovered an allied process, called transduction, in

one of these temperate viruses. Working with a virus that invades bacteria, Lederberg and Norton D. Zinder found that, in attaching itself to a bacterium's chromosomes, it often carried over fragments of bacterial DNA from other hosts, which became incorporated in the new strain through succeeding generations. Much research has now focused on this process as a means of effecting changes in human chromosomes. Biologists have found viruses that will carry a single gene or strip of genes from one organism to another, inserting it in the proper place in the DNA. At least one laboratory is reported to be grooming a suitable virus for the job of attempting the same risky experiment on man.

Computerizing the chromosomes

Dozens of laboratories, in fact, are pressing research on many fronts. The processes of transferring genes are steadily being made more efficient and specific. Variations on transduction, using episomes—mysterious small genetic particles found in cells—are being explored. And techniques for mapping the genetic structure of chromosomes are being developed to a fine art. It is no longer difficult to imagine the day when chromosome analysis will be a routine part of prenatal care, and DNA abnormalities will be corrected in the foetus before birth. Already, such analysis is a part of specialized medicine for diagnostic purposes, and scientists at Columbia–Presbyterian Medical Center in New York have joined with Avco Corp. in putting the first stages of the problem into a computer for the rapid scanning and analysis of human chromosomes. The computer, in fact, may well be a decisive tool in handling economically the enormous complexities of human heredity and genetic engineering.

Needless to say, the prospect of making small significant

changes in genetic characteristics, which is likely to be the first direct outcome of this initial stage of unlocking the genetic code in DNA, raises large ethical, legal, and social issues. For the same techniques that may correct genetic errors may also be used to effect other changes. At the present stage in genetic knowledge some of the effects could be unforeseeable, fatal, and even monstrous.

The philosophical consequences are clearly portentous. Though many people, including some biologists, still cling to the old vitalistic belief that there is at the core of life a forever mysterious force that will never be explained in physical terms, they are being given less and less ground to stand on.

2 *At the Controls of the Living Cell*

The ultimate mystery of life is how a single living cell, dividing and subdividing again and again, in the well-ordered drama of conception, birth, and development, becomes in time a complex, sentient organism such as man. For about a century, embryologists have wrestled with this great problem, gaining many insights into its depths but arriving at no firm conclusions as to exactly how life takes shape. Now, with the discovery that the genesis and control of all life lies in a unique, double-stranded, helical molecule known as deoxyribonucleic acid or DNA, biologists have opened the way to solving the central mystery.

In the first chapter, we saw DNA tracked down as

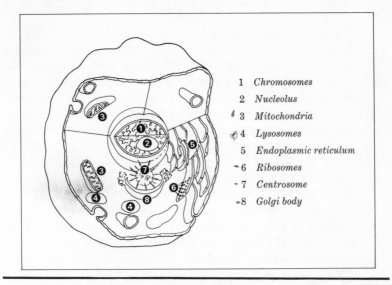

1 *Chromosomes*
2 *Nucleolus*
3 *Mitochondria*
4 *Lysosomes*
5 *Endoplasmic reticulum*
6 *Ribosomes*
7 *Centrosome*
8 *Golgi body*

The basic unit of life is the cell. What the atom is to all matter, this microcosm is to all living things, from the one-cell microorganisms up to man, who is built of a million million highly organized, interacting cells of many types. Nearly all cells have in common the major elements shown in this cutaway drawing. In the nucleus lie the coiled, twisted, and controlling chromosomes, with their double helical strands of DNA, and the nucleoli, believed to be storehouses of nucleic acid for the reproduction of DNA in cell division. Outside the nucleus is the cytoplasm, containing the cell's working parts, whose structure and distribution are controlled by the DNA.

The mitochondria are the cell's power plants, storing and releasing energy in complex molecular reactions. The lysosomes form a digestive apparatus that breaks down the cell when its usefulness is ended. The endoplasmic reticulum, a convoluted inner membrane, has many guidance and control functions; on it are clustered the ribosomes, the tiny granular sites of protein synthesis. The centrosome plays some undefined role in cell division, while the function of the Golgi body is as yet unknown. Enveloping everything is the cell wall or membrane, a complex structure that protects the inner works, selectively pumps materials in or out, and acts as a sensory apparatus.

the genetic material in the nucleus and chromosomes of living cells, and how it was found to possess in the ordered sequence of bases in its chemical structure a master code or blueprint specifying the exact form and function of each living organism. We also saw, in two elementary ways, how this code works. First, in cell division, DNA transmits the full code to succeeding cell generations by splitting its two strands apart and forming on the separated strands two exact replicas of itself. Thus DNA is the self-reproducing molecule responsible for the continuity of life. Second, DNA transmits its code by transcribing portions of it on a secondary, single-stranded form of ribonucleic acid called messenger RNA, which goes out into the cell to direct the formation of all the characteristic proteins making up the cell or organism. But while this DNA-RNA-protein synthesis explains how individual genes direct the production of specific proteins, it does not explain how many genes acting in concert give rise to a complex new organism.

The older genetics had long ago settled on the general laws by which new life is born. In nearly all higher forms of life, above the one-cell organisms, reproduction takes place not by simple cell division but by a sexual joining of parental chromosomes to form a new combination. The chromosomes of all higher organisms come in two complete, duplicate sets. In reproduction, one set of chromosomes from the father and one from the mother are joined together by means of special sex cells containing only half of each parent's chromosomes. Each set may come from the parent's paternal or its maternal side, and in the act of joining, the composition of the chromosome sets may be further reshuffled by a mysterious process called recombination or crossover, in which some gene groups are broken apart and exchanged between pairs of chromosomes. Thus an immense diversity of traits is assured, within species limits, in the single-cell fertilized egg.

From the moment of fertilization an almost magical process takes place. In the explosive growth of millions of cells from a single cell (see page 32), an entirely new organism gradually takes shape. This development proceeds in well-marked phases, almost with the precision of a preset program. At first the embryo is just a blob of cells hardly distinguishable from one another, then the cells begin to be segregated in slightly different regions, and finally recognizable features of an organism appear.

The program directing this development is written, as we now know, in the DNA contained in the chromosomes. It is written in the endlessly variable order of four simple organic chemicals in DNA's structure, designating, in triplet sequences or code "words," the order in which some twenty amino acids are to be built by the cell into specific proteins. With these physical units in hand, it is possible to get to the bottom of the mysterious process of recombination and of conception itself. More important, the new knowledge allows the great central question of development to be asked with more point and precision. If each embryonic cell contains in its nucleus a full replica of the DNA designating the whole organism, then how is it that some cells become muscle and bone, while others become brain, nerve, liver, kidney, spleen, and all the other quite different bundles of specialized cells that make up a man?

It is this question that is currently occupying the most active frontier of molecular biology. This new frontier is concerned with nothing less than the organization and control of whole organs and the total organism, involving the interactions of many genes with the cell environment. A fuller understanding of these interactions will lead to much more fundamental knowledge of how the human body works, how diseases affect it, and how drugs act upon it. Potentially within grasp is the first basic understanding of such processes as immunization, viral infection, and aging,

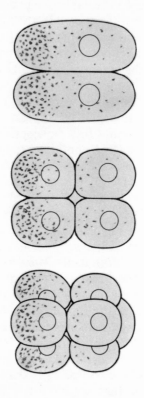

Life begins with a single-cell egg, which divides into two, then into four, and so on, until a complex organism develops. After each division the cells become increasingly differentiated. When the cells divide, as this drawing shows, certain elements in their cytoplasm are distributed unevenly to their offspring, foreshadowing different lines of development. Somehow the genes in the DNA must be turned on and off to produce different types of cell from a single precursor. One theory of how this works is shown on page 36.

and of such widespread degenerative disorders as hypertension, heart disease, and cancer.

A computer-operated chemical plant

At the center of this new quest for knowledge is the cell, the basic structural unit of life. Cell theory, like genetic theory, was formulated in the last century, by two prescient German biologists, Matthias J. Schleiden and Theodor Schwann, long before most of the physical parts of the cell were known. Only in the last two decades or so, however, with the development of such instruments and techniques as the electron microscope, the ultracentrifuge, and radioactive tracers, have biologists been able to view the complex components of this fundamental unit as a functioning whole.

In the nineteenth century, under the spell of the early industrial revolution, the cell was most often likened to a factory. A more sophisticated analogy today would be a completely automatic electrochemical plant run by a central computer—the DNA of the chromosomes. Packed into this tiny plant is a maze of circuitry, energy-conversion, information-transfer, and processing devices that makes the most advanced of today's microelectronics look crude indeed. A million human cells, for instance, could be put on the head of a pin. And even a one-cell organism carries on hundreds of intricate chemical reactions, side by side, without confusion. Most of the major reactions, such as the one in which energy is stored and released in complex molecules through the respiratory oxidation of sugars and fats, are many-stage cyclic reactions. The product of one stage initiates the next, with the aid of specific enzymes, until in the final stage a product is produced that starts the cycle over again. Reactions proceed at different times and different rates, some only at special times or intermittently. A set of exquisite controls must therefore be at work, keeping the cell in equilibrium, producing not too much of one product or too little of another, to sustain the orderly processes of growth and development.

The simplest of these controls, biochemists early found, is a form of negative "feedback" control common in chemical engineering and electronics. When an excess of end product appears, it reacts back upon the start of the process to inhibit production. Extensive experiments have now shown that in the cell this may work in one of two ways: the excess product may lock molecularly into control sites on the activating enzymes, making them inactive; or the product may join somehow with the messenger RNA responsible for synthesizing the enzymes, cutting off their further production. While this feedback system may account for much of the local control of individual reactions, it does not begin to answer the major question. How, in a basic way, are a great number of processes turned on and off and coordinated in the variety of cells making up a complex organism? Ultimately, a great loop of feedback controls must extend back to the DNA in the cell nucleus.

The rebels at the Pasteur Institute

The first glimmer of a master control system appeared in a notable review paper in 1961 titled "Genetic Regulatory Mechanisms in the Synthesis of Proteins," by François Jacob and Jacques Monod of the Pasteur Institute of Paris. Jacob and Monod, who had been Free French and Resistance fighters throughout World War II, came to the Pasteur Institute after the war, and in the laboratory of André Lwoff, a noted microbiologist, took up the new molecular biology, particularly the study of enzyme synthesis in bacteria. By 1960 their own and others' experiments had piled up many odd bits and pieces of evidence of how enzyme synthesis is induced and repressed in these one-cell creatures. So they sat down to try to bring some theoretical order out of the then abounding confusion.

Jacob and Monod first proposed that DNA transcribes a section of its code specifying a particular enzyme on a short-lived, mobile molecule that then goes out to act as a template upon which the protein is formed. Such a molecule, in fact, had been identified by U.S. biologists even before their paper appeared, and it became known as messenger RNA. Jacob and Monod's thesis was that DNA production of such a molecule sharply controls enzyme production. They then went on to suggest in a more far-reaching way how this control works. DNA, they postulated, contains two kinds of genes: structural genes that specify the formation of specific proteins and, some distance away from these on the DNA chain, regulator genes that act upon the structural genes, controlling their production of messenger RNA. The molecular make-up of each structural gene had at its starting point a short DNA-coded sequence that triggered gene action. Jacob and Monod called this coded sequence the operator, and the combination of operator and structural gene, an operon. Since information or orders can be transmitted in a chemical system only through the physical shape of specific molecules, they proposed two additional entities to make the control system work: a repressor and an inducer substance. The regulator gene, they theorized, produced a specific repressor that bound itself to the operator, preventing it from triggering the operon into synthesizing messenger RNA. The operator was released, and RNA synthesis proceeded, when an inducer—a small specialized molecule or metabolite—disengaged the repressor and allowed the operon to function.

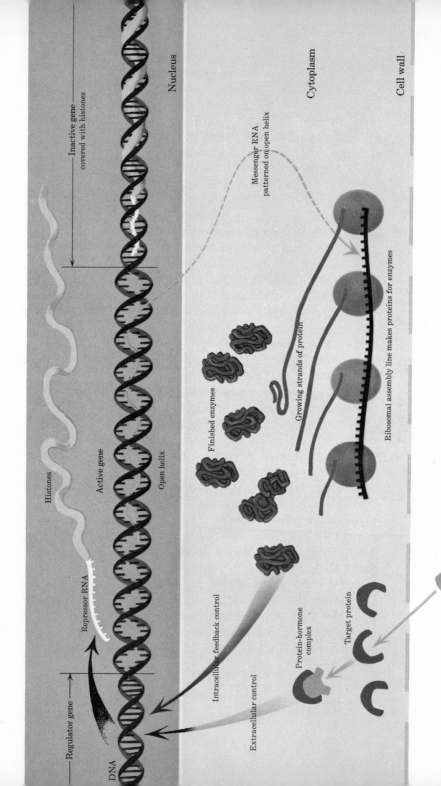

Nucleus

Cytoplasm

Cell wall

Inactive gene
covered with histones

Messenger RNA
patterned on open helix

Histones

Active gene

Open helix

Finished enzymes

Growing strands of protein

Ribosomal assembly line makes proteins for enzymes

Repressor RNA

Intracellular feedback control

Protein-hormone
complex

Regulator gene

Extracellular control

Target protein

DNA

Hormone from other cells

How genes are switched on and off

The process by which genes are activated and deactivated is complex and not yet wholly understood. This diagram illustrates some recent speculations. The basic theory is that the genes which direct the structural formation of specific proteins are themselves controlled by so-called regulator genes. These exercise control through special repressor and inducer substances that respectively lock and unlock the structural genes. In higher organisms these substances have been found to be mainly histones and hormones, two classes of complex molecules. In the DNA strand above, the gene at right has a chain of histones wound tightly around it, preventing it from transcribing messenger RNA to make protein. One theory is that the histone chain is guided to the gene by a specific repressor RNA, made by its regulator gene, as illustrated at top center. The repressor is released by a hormone that moves into the cell from a distant gland (lower left). This hormone finds and activates a target protein, which then disengages the repressor chain of histones, allowing the DNA to synthesize RNA to make a protein enzyme (bottom center). Enzyme production in turn is controlled by an internal feedback mechanism. When an excessive amount of enzyme is produced it reacts back on the regulator to repress the gene again.

For the promulgation of this so-called operon theory, which presented microbiologists with a new vocabulary and a range of new ideas with which to experiment, Jacob and Monod in 1965 received the Nobel Prize, along with Lwoff, who had made many basic contributions to the understanding of gene operation in viruses and bacteria. It was France's first Nobel Prize in science in thirty years. Monod seized the occasion to launch a blistering attack upon a rigid, minister-dominated educational system, laid down by Napoleon, which had sapped innovation and was experiencing no improvement under another rigid military man, de Gaulle. Monod's group had waged a long struggle to conduct its research, which was unrecognized in the classical curriculum of the universities, given only limited recognition by the French Academy of Sciences, and even hampered by the administration of the Pasteur Institute. Monod's attack sparked an upheaval in the institute second only to the commotion loosed in biological circles by the operon theory itself.

In a fever of experimentation, parts of the theory have been confirmed, parts remain to be proved, and the whole is still a subject of some controversy. The validity of the operon concept has been demonstrated, through experiments involving controlled mutations, in many types of bacteria. Its operation has been fitted to the action of many well-known inducers, mainly key substances or substrates of the reactions to be induced. For instance, when a molecule of the milk sugar, lactose, is presented to a specific repressed operon, the operon is immediately unlocked and begins making messenger RNA to produce the enzyme needed to break down lactose. In the absence of lactose, the operon is again repressed. The location of the regulator genes that effect this repression also has been confirmed, through genetic mapping techniques, but the nature of the repressor substance itself is still unknown, and the whole regulatory mechanism remains obscure.

Because there are these gaps, many biologists believe that the operon theory will be found to apply only to certain genetic sites, and only to bacteria, whose cells are all alike and simple. It can only begin to suggest the much more definite and elaborate control apparatus required for multicell higher organisms.

"Seeing-eye-dog RNA"

The chromosomes of higher plants, insects, animals, and man were early found to differ in one important respect from those of bacteria and other one-cell organisms. Besides being bigger, more numerous, and more complex, the higher chromosomes had an ingredient never found in bacteria—a complex of nucleoproteins called histones. Indeed, these proteins were discovered in close association with DNA by the Swiss chemist J. Friedrich Miescher nearly a century ago. But since no one had any idea what purpose they served, both the histones and DNA remained merely curious chemical compounds. About 1950, however, with DNA finally identified as the genetic material, two British biochemists, Edgar Stedman and his wife Ellen, took another look at the histones and suggested they might somehow act as gene inhibitors. The suggestion was ignored for several years. Then the rapid unraveling of the DNA code and the rise of the operon theory impelled a number of laboratories to take off after the histones.

A group at the California Institute of Technology, led by James Bonner and Ru-chih Huang, conducted a series of elegant experiments on pea-plant chromosomes—the classic subject of Mendel's original genetic observations a century ago. By 1963 the Caltech team had demonstrated that histones appeared to be the main repressors of gene action in multicell organisms. They isolated the chromosomes and showed that in their natural state they synthesized only 5 to 20 percent as much messenger RNA as chromosomes from which all histones had been removed. Some 80 to 95 percent of the DNA in the chromosomes, they found, was covered by histones, blocking RNA synthesis. They then focused on one gene responsible for storing a specific protein in pea seeds. This gene operated only in pea seeds during growth, and in no other part of the plant at any time, though the gene was present but dormant in all the other plant cells. This they demonstrated by removing histones from the chromosomes of bud cells, whereupon the bud-cell chromosomes were induced to produce seed protein.

At about the same time a group at Rockefeller University in New York, led by Vincent G. Allfrey and Alfred E. Mirsky, reported an extensive series of related experiments on the nuclear chromosomes of calf thymus-gland cells. They showed that adding free histones to the isolated nuclei substantially cut down their synthesis of RNA, and, conversely, that selectively stripping histones from the nuclear chromosomes greatly increased RNA production. Later Allfrey showed that histones varied in their repressing activity according to how strongly they bonded themselves to the DNA, and this depended in turn on the degree of acetylation in the histone molecules.

Meanwhile, Bonner and his group went on to make an ever more detailed physicochemical study of histones. They found that histones worked in much the same way in cows, rats, insects, and humans as they did in peas. In all these organisms they found that histone complexes blanketed 80 to 95 percent of the chromosomal DNA, but in different regions on the chromosomes of different cells, as was to be expected in cells having various specialized structures and purposes. Only the genes needed for a particular cell or organ were left free to operate. They also concluded that there are only five types of histones, common to all higher organisms, and that these wrap themselves around the DNA and adhere to it with various degrees of bond strength. Finally, they came upon what may be an answer to the most puzzling of all questions concerning histones: how do they know which genes to sit on and which to leave alone? The histones do not come in enough structural varieties to be selective, and no one has been able to discover that they bond themselves to DNA by anything but simple electrostatic attraction. In the summer of 1965 Bonner and Huang discovered what they believe is a new form of RNA, attached to long chains of histones of one type. Presumably made by a regulator gene and therefore specifically coded, this RNA tag might act as a guide—Bonner whimsically calls it "seeing-eye-dog RNA"—drawing its chain of histones to a specific site on a structural gene, where it clamps on by simple attraction.

Hands on the genetic throttle

At the same time that the histones were being run down, a hunt was also on for the inducers that release these repressors. A major candidate soon turned up in another old but more familiar class of compounds—the hormones. These complex protein and hybrid molecules, secreted by special glands, long had been known for their ability to move about in the body and selectively influence distant cells and tissues. Their powerfully stimulating, multiple effects on cell activity, as seen in the performance of insulin and the sex hormones, had already made them useful in modern medicine. But little was known about how they really worked until molecular biologists began to look at them in the new context. The nature of the hormonal action has come into focus only in the last two or three years, under the scrutiny of many laboratories, from the Max Planck Institute for Biology in West Germany to the University of California School of Medicine at Los Angeles. It is now generally evident that the hormones act as the main releasers or inducers of genetic action in higher organisms.

The general pattern of experiments by which this was

proved involved administering a specific hormone to test animals, and then measuring at intervals the rate of protein synthesis it induced in certain target cells, hence the rate at which the DNA in these cells was producing RNA. In one instance, protein production started to rise within thirty minutes after hormone injection and soon jumped as much as 300 percent. Then, as a clincher, a further experiment was performed. It was based on the discovery, early in the research on gene activity, that some antibiotics temporarily block all DNA manufacture of RNA. Indeed, this turned out to be one of the basic ways in which antibiotics work; they deny to an infecting organism the supply of cellular enzymes and other proteins it needs in order to grow. So, as a final check on how the hormone acts, test animals were given an antibiotic known to block all RNA production. When the hormone was administered to these animals, it had no effect at all. This proved that the hormone acts upon DNA at the gene level.

The exact mode of hormone action is not yet quite clear. One general theory is that a hormone, entering a cell, combines with or activates a waiting target protein, which then goes to a specific site on the DNA to disengage the repressive histones, thus uncovering the genes so they can make RNA. But this is not the only way hormones work. Some hormones have been found to activate enzymes directly to make more protein, while others have been discovered attached to cell walls, regulating the passage of such elements as salt across cell membranes. Nor are hormones the only inducers of gene activity. A host of metabolites and other agents, such as the sunlight that wakes a green leaf's chlorophyll to action, are known to unlock the genes in many metabolic systems. Level upon level of controls are needed to ensure that the right proteins are made in the right amounts at the right time. But in the discovery of how hormones and histones act, biologists at last have their hands upon the main throttles that turn genes on and off.

How a plant decides to flower

Still to be explained, however, is the great central process by which DNA controls the development of many different types of cells from a single precursor to form a complete, complex organism. Biologists call this process differentiation. It is so delicately tuned that a plant produces its flower and fruit precisely in season, and each feature of the human form takes shape and grows only so big and no bigger. The basic mechanism, as we have seen, is the switching off of some genes and the turning on of others in sequence, so as to produce different types of cells for different purposes. But what is it that selects the right genes to repress and the right ones to activate in these differentiated cells—each of which contains, be it remembered, the full DNA code of the organism?

To begin to think about the problem, Bonner and his group at Caltech have set up a computer program to try to simulate, in a simplified way, the logical stages by which a single apical cell at the tip of a growing plant continuously divides and gives rise to a bud, stem tissue, and finally a flower. At each cell division, Bonner reasoned, the growing cells must test themselves for position and proximity to neighboring cells. If a cell finds itself all alone at the very tip of a stem, it concludes it is the apical cell and continues to divide. (Frederick C. Steward of Cornell has shown that if any one cell of a carrot plant is isolated and nurtured, it proceeds to act like an apical cell and grows into a whole new plant.) If a cell finds itself surrounded by neighbors, then it concludes it is a bud cell, some of its genes are turned off, and further growth is inhibited. (Cells have been shown to have a means, through cell-wall contacts, of identifying and influencing one another in development; in the course of differentiation they manufacture a special mucilage that causes like cells to stick together, inhibiting growth.)

43

As the bud swells under the ever dividing apical cell, older cells near the bud's surface and base enter a second stage of differentiation and become leaf and stem tissue. At this point another round of self-testing and turning on and off of genes takes place. If, for instance, a bud cell near the base finds one surface exposed to air, it develops into an epidermal cell; if it finds itself inside a cell mass, it becomes xylem, the pithy inner structure of the stem.

Bonner translated all these events into computer language so that he could test out his logical assumptions of what happened at each stage of the plant's development. He has still to work out a computer program for flowering. Experiments have shown that this takes place when the leaves of the mature plant "notice" that daylight is lasting a certain length of time. They thereupon release a hormone that goes to the bud, where it unlocks the genes that control flowering.

"The development process behaves as though it were a pre-programed routine, a pre-programed sequence written down in the genetic DNA," says Bonner. It is a process that, once started on a pathway or on a subroutine such as flowering, flows on almost automatically. Yet it is also a process in which there is a constant feedback of information to the nuclear DNA from the cell's cytoplasm, cell walls, and the environment that triggers, paces, and even modifies the stages of development. A steady flow of information and stimulation, particularly in the initial stages of differentiation, is required to evoke the genes to proper development. Bonner believes that the computer may help in understanding this complicated interplay, if only because it forces biologists to think through the development process more rigorously in order to program it.

Creative federalism in the cell

Many laboratories are now beginning to get at these dual aspects of differentiation—the action of the genetic code and the reaction of the environment—by working on living embryos. One of the leading investigators is Eric H. Davidson, a young assistant in Alfred Mirsky's laboratory at Rockefeller University, who is working on embryos of the curious marine snail, *Ilyanassa*. Over half a century ago embryologists discovered through the study of various creatures, including *Ilyanassa*, that egg cells contain in their cytoplasm mysterious, unevenly distributed, localized "factors" that seem to determine how various regions of the cell will develop. The snail *Ilyanassa* was selected for study because, before cell division, its eggs take on a convenient trefoil form. One of the three lobes of the trefoil contains none of the egg cell's genetic material, and hence it could easily be lopped off to study how the organism develops without part of its original cytoplasm. The dismembered cell grew into a wriggling, free-swimming creature, but with some of its most important tissues missing. No one knew why.

Davidson returned to the study of *Ilyanassa* with all the newfound knowledge of how DNA functions. He showed that removal of the lobe eventually causes the embryo's rate of RNA synthesis, and hence its protein production, to drop below normal, precisely at the stage of cell differentiation when gene activity usually rises dramatically. The inescapable conclusion is that some important genes are left repressed and inactive in the absence of the cytoplasmic factors contained in the missing lobe. This conclusion is being fortified by similar microsurgical experiments on the eggs of the toad *Xenopus*. In addition, the work on *Xenopus* is demonstrating that the genes left inactive by cytoplasmic surgery are fully capable of activation.

Thus the cytoplasm of the egg cell is being viewed more and more as the crux of development. Laid down in this jelly-like fluid during the cell's long maturation in the maternal body is a rich store of special factors without which the orderly sequences of development and differentiation cannot take place. These factors are still unknown, but are probably trace-able to specialized RNA and protein inducers specified by the maternal DNA. As some scientists now see it, the cell is a kind of federation, in which the nuclear DNA of the chromosomes acts as the central government, while certain elements of the cytoplasm operate as semi-autonomous states. Recent studies have shown, for instance, that such particles as the mitochon-dria, the power plants of the cell, have a small, non-nuclear DNA component in their own makeup. The DNA of the chromosomes remains in strong, central control, but the rest of the cell, the whole organism, and the total environment all have a critical say in development. The task of unraveling these subtle interrelationships in the human egg cell will be a vast one for many investigators. But the basic principles are at hand, a start has been made, and progress should be rapid.

Toward a molecular medicine

Out of this rapidly broadening base of new knowledge may come developments as varied and spectacular as life itself. One of the earliest and most predictable will be a great ex-pansion in the synthesis and use of hormones or other meta-bolic agents to intervene more precisely in the activation of specific genes controlling body processes. Great developments have already taken place in this field, notably the introduc-tion of such hormonal agents as the birth-control pills, but the surface has only been scratched.

Back in 1965 a successful experiment was reported by M. James Whitelaw of San Jose, California, who used a cortisone-like hormone to reduce a hereditary tendency to excessive tallness in fifty teen-age girls. The hormone accelerated puberty so as to shorten the growth period, keeping the girls' heights an estimated two to six inches below their ultimate theoretical growth. Not only height but body build may someday be regulated in the same way. And only in 1965 a team at London's Postgraduate Medical School reported that a newly discovered thyroid hormone, named thyrocalcitonin, sharply controls excess calcium in the blood, seemingly by depositing it in bone. The behavior of this hormone may go far to explain and treat certain bone diseases, including bone cancer, in which calcium from bone is lost to the blood. Many more hormones and their intricate pathways in the body remain to be discovered.

There is also likely to be sharply rising interest in the synthesis of inhibitors or blocking agents to curb gene activities that have got out of control. For instance, man has inherited from primitive ancestors a genetic "fight or flight" mechanism that swiftly pours adrenal hormones into the bloodstream to meet any sudden danger. These agents, chiefly epinephrine, secreted in the inner part of the adrenal glands, powerfully step up the heart beat, dilate some arteries, and constrict others, to send a massive flow of blood to the muscles for instant physical action. This mechanism is no longer widely needed in civilized life, but it continues to be triggered in some individuals by less tangible threats, fears, and frustrations, leading in some cases to chronic high blood pressure and heart attacks. Two classes of chemical compounds have now been found to short-circuit this mechanism. One is an agent that blocks epinephrine action on the arteries; the other, more recently discovered by scientists of the Lilly research laboratories, blocks epinephrine excitation of the heart muscle. At the same time, the National Heart Institute is pressing a search further back in the genetic system to find a means of curbing the production of adrenal hormones themselves by inhibiting a key enzyme in their synthesis. Most of the solutions to heart and arterial diseases seem to lie in these devious pathways of genetic control.

The most striking example of the genetic system's getting out of control is, of course, cancer. In this malady the cells of an organ or tissue become unstuck, so that their growth is no longer regulated by contact with other cells. They then wildly multiply and degenerate back toward an undifferentiated state. Much of the basic research on DNA and molecular biology is being supported by cancer research funds, for cancer involves in a basic way the derangement of the central repressor and inducer mechanism of DNA. Any deeper understanding of this basic mechanism will aid in tracking down the causes not only of cancer but of a host of other degenerative diseases—and aid in developing the drugs to control them. The implication of viruses, those infectious threads of DNA or RNA, in the stealthy triggering of certain types of cancer grows stronger by the day. And drug research is piling up so many promising leads that the National Cancer Institute, for the first time, is entering into industrial research contracts to run them down more quickly.

The lock and key of the body's defenses

Meanwhile, stirring progress is being made in clarifying the body's basic defense system itself. This work focuses upon the antibodies, those long mysterious protein agents that are manufactured by special plasma cells and arise in magical numbers to repel a disease invader or any foreign substance, providing future immunity against it. Only in the past few years, through work carried on in many laboratories, has the detailed structure of the antibodies become known. The antibody is a large, elongated molecule, composed of four subunit chains, joined in such a way that at both ends of the molecule there are identically shaped "slots" that fit and lock upon a specific invader, or antigen. Laborious step-by-step analysis revealed that the main sections of all antibodies of a particular class have a common amino-acid sequence, and hence are controlled by a single gene. But the end sections, bearing the specifically shaped slots, differ from antibody to antibody. When all the various end-section sequences are translated back into the DNA code, it looks strongly as though each distinctive shape was made by a different gene. As many as 10,000 different genes might be needed, if this is so, to arm a sufficient variety of antibodies to meet the range of possible disease invaders.

Several theories have been put forward to explain the unique composite structure of the antibody, which seems to violate the dictum that one gene controls the production of one protein chain. One such theory was proposed in 1965 by William J. Dreyer and J. Claude Bennett of Caltech, who focused on the primitive plasma cell that makes antibodies. They maintained that as each plasma cell goes through the process of differentiation it combines one common gene with one of the genes that specifies a particular end shape; it leaves all the rest of the end-shape genes turned off. That cell can then make only one kind of antibody. Each primitive plasma cell is preset to make a different antibody and it then lies dormant until it is invaded by a foreign agent that fits—e.g., a specific virus—whereupon the cell jumps into action, vigorously dividing and pouring out large amounts of the specific antibody to overcome the invasion. Thus plasma cells may be the most widely differentiated cells in the body, genetically pooling all the antibody shapes devised by living organisms over eons of time and evolution to protect themselves.

With this growing knowledge of antibody structure and how it is put together, scientists may soon be making antibodies in the laboratory and thus mobilizing a powerful new agent against disease. Dreyer thinks such a step may be only a few years away. Ultimately it may be possible to build up resistance to disease in a more basic way. The resistance to disease varies widely in human populations. Some people, for instance, seem to have a hereditary resistance to tuberculosis or cancer, while others do not, because they have a deficiency in antibody production. It may be possible to correct this deficiency by implantation of specific plasma cells or by correction of the genes themselves.

"I would like to have four hands"

When scientists let their imaginations reach out from this new body of knowledge, they go much further than this. They believe it may be possible to intervene genetically in the development of tissues and organs themselves. In highly complex animals differentiation is normally irreversible. Once a man's cells are set in a specialized way, he cannot regrow lost parts or generate new ones, as less highly differentiated creatures do; a lizard, for example, can regrow a lost tail, or a plant may generate new roots or branches from most of its parts. But James Bonner, for one, thinks that now that biologists have the key to turning genes on and off, they should be able to take any human cell and reset its program at will to any stage in the developmental process. It may become possible, for instance, to cure diabetics by resetting and reactivating the genes responsible for making insulin, which have become repressed through degenerative disease. It is even conceivable that whole genetic programs can be reset to replace tired or damaged organs, or to generate entirely new or additional ones.

"I have tried to think about what further organs I would like to have," says Bonner, only half jokingly, "and I have decided that I would like to have four hands, since there is so much for biologists to do. Recently, as I was trying to light my pipe in the laboratory, my colleague, Professor Huang, said to me, 'If you're going to smoke a pipe in the laboratory you'll need five.' "

An even more immediately promising prospect is the transplantation of whole organs. The basic obstacle to such transplantation is that antibody action automatically rejects all grafts of foreign tissue. But scientists are very close to finding a way around this barrier through increasing knowledge of the immunological process. Another line of research is exploring ways to make damaged organs repair themselves. In 1960, Ruth Hill of Columbia University, studying the effects of ultraviolet radiation on viruses and bacteria, found a clue to the existence of a self-repair mechanism. It cut out radiation-damaged genes and replaced them with new ones in the living DNA. Groups working under Paul Howard-Flanders at Yale University and Richard B. Setlow at Oak Ridge National Laboratory have now worked out the essential details of this repair mechanism, which is controlled by three genes and their resulting enzymes. A similar mechanism, operating in man, may help him to survive in a world of increasing radioactivity and space travel. Howard-Flanders and others have gone on to suggest that this repair mechanism may also be the means by which recombination takes place in the fertilization of egg cells in higher organisms. Thus a fuller understanding of the mechanism may not only show how it might be used to make repairs in man's chromosomes, but it could also reveal the great secret of how chromosomes recombine in human conception.

Intervening in human heredity

A number of bold experimenters in the U.S. and Europe are pressing into this mysterious realm. Robert G. Edwards, who works both at Johns Hopkins Hospital in Baltimore and at Cambridge University, England, has succeeded for the first time in growing human eggs outside the body, up through what appears to be the stage of fertilization. At birth the female ovaries contain some 500,000 potential ova, one of which normally matures each month during the childbearing period. Edwards obtains his eggs from ovaries that have been removed from women for medical reasons. There is no inherent reason why such eggs, given the right laboratory environment—a big order—cannot be grown up to the stage of a full-term fetus.

At the same time, Teh Ping Lin of the University of California School of Medicine in San Francisco has developed a technique for removing and delicately injecting minute amounts of material into fertilized mouse eggs—which are only ten times larger than a human red blood cell—and then reimplanting them in foster mothers, where some continue to grow into normal embryos. Together these two techniques offer the possibility of manipulating the human egg outside the body and of introducing specific materials to influence its genetic development, for instance, altering sex characteristics.

No complete account can be given of the numerous paths and bypaths down which the revolution in molecular biology is moving. If, as has been amply demonstrated, all genetic information is stored in the four simple organic chemical bases of DNA, then it follows that all of life's complexity and variety, all its patterns of behavior, and all mental traits and abilities are basically open to study and manipulation. There is no ironbound tyranny in the genes. A new light has been thrown on the old controversy of genetic inheritance versus environment. For it is now reaffirmed on the deepest molecular level that the individual genes cannot develop fully without the right physical environment and stimulation. In addition to learning how to manipulate the genes, therefore, we may also learn how to awaken the great pool of dormant genes that lies untapped in the human race.

3 *Inside the Molecules of the Mind*

The recent great discoveries made in molecular biology are beginning to cast a truly portentous light on the deepest levels of the human brain. For the first time, science seems to be within reach of understanding not only the physicochemical workings of the brain and nervous system, but also the mysteries of consciousness, memory, learning, and other mental processes. This new knowledge could open an entirely new era in man's history. Obviously, it could have immense implications for all education and for the conquest of mental diseases. But beyond that loom ways of heightening or enlarging, modifying or controlling men's mental capacities and drives. No less awesome are the potential dangers—already worrisome to the scientists involved—of thus intervening genetically in the mainspring of man's being.

The physical basis of this explosive new development was laid down when it was found that the total genetic information governing the form and function of every living cell and organism is chemically coded in giant linear molecules of deoxyribonucleic acid or DNA. This information is transferred in short sequences, as needed, to strips of ribonucleic acid or RNA, which act as templates for molding the thousands of specific proteins making up a particular cell or organism. In the embryonic development of complex organisms such as man, different gene sequences are switched on and off in different cells, according to a program laid down in the DNA and cytoplasm of the egg cell, to form the different specialized tissues and organs of the human body. Just as the DNA code determines the color of the eye, the shape of the nose, and the precise operations of such complex organs as the liver, so it also determines the cast of the mind. The new hypothesis is that DNA not only specifies the physical structure of the brain, but it also controls, directly or indirectly, all brain processes and mental activity through a molecular code that may be searched out and finally mastered.

So far only two or three suggestive links have been found between DNA and brain activity, and the whole hypothesis is in a swirl of controversy. But enough has emerged to excite in molecular biologists a feeling that this is the next great area of research and discovery. A dozen heated symposia have discussed the subject in the last few years. One of the biggest drew a packed house at the December, 1965, annual meeting of the American Association for the Advancement of Science. And the Massachusetts

Institute of Technology has set up a unique interdisciplinary center and clearinghouse, called the Neurosciences Research Program, to begin to coordinate the flood of data flowing from biochemical, biophysical, genetic, neurological, pharmacological, and psychological laboratories. "Whether one likes it or not," says Francis O. Schmitt, the chairman of the program, "man has embarked on the greatest of human experiments."

Brain waves vs. "brain hash"

For over half a century scientists have been poking and probing the human brain, the most complex and tantalizing of all organs. Anatomists estimate that the brain alone, not including the great connecting maze of the peripheral nervous system, contains some 10 billion nerve cells or neurons. These in turn are sheathed or supported by some 100 billion glial cells, little noticed until recently. The main operative unit is the neuron, the most remarkable of specialized cells. It is further differentiated into three broad types: motor neurons, which spark the contraction of muscles; sensory neurons, which receive and transmit light, heat, pressure, and other sense impulses; and interneurons, the most numerous, which interconnect the more specialized types and make up the brain. All neurons are interconnected, and in the tightly packed convolutions of the brain the connections to and from each neuron run into the thousands, producing a network of unsurpassed mystery and complexity.

The electrical nature of nerve impulses has been known ever since Luigi Galvani made his celebrated observations of the twitching of severed frogs' legs about 1790. But little was learned in detail until 1924, when, by a notable coincidence, Hans Berger in Austria invented the electro-encephalograph for recording brain waves from the surface of man's skull, and Walter R. Hess in Switzerland devised a method for implanting electrodes deep in the brain of animals to study brain regions selectively. Using these instruments, which have dominated brain research up to now, a long line of brilliant experimenters have established that the brain is suffused by a steady, low-voltage background wave, called the alpha rhythm, which changes pattern with alertness, drowsiness, concentration, and specific sensory excitations. Through studies of these wave patterns, the mysteries of sleep and dreaming, and of such disorders as epilepsy, have been deeply investigated for the first time. By carefully implanting electrodes and exciting nets of neurons, experimenters have located with some precision the brain's motor and homeostatic control centers, visual and auditory centers, and the location of such built-in responses as aggression, fear, and rage. A major achievement in this line was the more precise mapping by Wilder Penfield of the Montreal Neurological Institute of the speech-control centers of the brain, which are intimately associated with the cerebral cortex, site of all the higher thought processes in man. More recent was the discovery by James Olds, then at McGill University in Montreal, of the brain's "pleasure" centers, which may be the most basic of all, since they underlie most of the organism's fundamental drives.

Parallel with this, biochemists began trying to determine the chemical processes and products of the brain by mincing and analyzing brain tissue. Neurons, they reasoned, carried on metabolism and protein synthesis like all other cells, but to the specialized end of producing nerve impulses. For a long time, the neurologists studying brain waves disparaged and ignored this "brain hash" chemistry, holding that all the significant operations of neurons were entirely electrical. As a matter of fact, the brain compounds isolated by chemists seemed to have such random, bewildering effects that, in the absence of a unified concept of how brain cells worked, they did not appear to fit into any logical scheme of operations. Yet a number of powerful substances were discovered, such as acetylcholine and serotonin, which seemed to be intimately involved in the speed and efficiency with which nerve impulses are transmitted. In addition, the actions of some specific hormones on the brain were traced. And compounds were finally isolated or developed that acted upon brain centers almost as specifically as electrical probes.

Gradually the chemical and electrical camps came together. Today no doubt remains that the underlying operation of the neuron (see illustrations pp. 64–67) is electrochemical. Clinching evidence came in the 1950's when it was proved that the critical transmission of nerve impulses from one neuron to another, across a membranous gap called a synapse, is accomplished by chemical transmitter substances. This work, which involved the dexterous use of the electron microscope and an ingenious new microelectrode technique for probing single nerve cells, was done by Sir John Eccles and his associates at the Australian National University at Canberra. So far only one transmitter substance has been positively identified—acetylcholine—but evidence suggests there are a large number of these specialized compounds keyed to the various types and gradations of nerve action.

Brilliant and basic as this work has been in tracing the mechanisms of neuron action, none of it went very far to explain the operation of complex networks of neurons in sorting, storing, shifting, and integrating information from the outer world. Speech centers were found, for instance, but not the places where words are stored, nor the areas where all the wonders and subtleties of spoken or written language take form. Only recently the noted British neurophysiologist W. Grey Walter wrote: "Since the days of the early Greek philosophers, who considered the brain as a radiator for overheated animal spirits and placed the mind in the diaphragm, the mechanisms of the brain have been almost inaccessible." In investigating all the higher cerebral areas, modern neurologists and psychologists have been limited up to now to inferring inner function from gross outward behavior, and some of their conjectures have proved to be not much nearer the mark than those of the early Greeks.

Patterns woven by "an enchanted loom"

The mechanism of memory has had a peculiar fascination because it underlies all learning and imaginative cognition in man. As was the case in the earlier theory of the neuron, the first substantial modern theory of memory, widely held until only a few years ago, was that it is an entirely electrical phenomenon. According to this theory, nerve impulses from the sensory system set up memory traces or pathways over synapses in the brain's network, and, depending on their strength or repetition, establish reverberating circuits for later recall. This theory was enshrined by the late, great British physiologist Sir Charles Sherrington in a phrase likening the brain to "an enchanted loom where millions of flashing shuttles weave a dissolving pattern."

Illustrating the dangers of lyricism, however, this theory was later in large part disproved. Various test animals were thoroughly taught new tasks, then given violent electroconvulsive shocks, powerful drugs, or other agents to disrupt or knock out all brain-wave patterns, but upon recovery they still remembered their new skills. Carefully trained mice were put in temperatures below freezing, where practically all electrical activity ceases, then thawed out, but they still retained their memories. Memory has a residue of permanency that no amount of short-circuiting, even to the extent of major brain damage, can erase.

A wealth of experimental and observational data now supports a three-level theory of memory. On the first level is short-term memory, on the order of a few seconds' duration or less. It is exemplified by the hundreds of sensory impressions flowing in upon the brain every waking second, most of which are promptly forgotten. On the second level is medium-term memory, with a duration ranging from a few minutes up to a few hours. It is demonstrated by such things as the retention of a telephone number only long enough to dial it, or cramming for an exam. At the deepest level is long-term memory. From all the sensory impressions and information flowing in, the cortex sifts and selects the data that, because of its vividness, interest, or usefulness, it chooses to preserve.

This memory takes time to register itself permanently, as has been shown in more refined experiments on animals as well as on men. If rats are given a strong electroshock immediately after first acquiring a new skill, all memory of the skill is erased. If the shock is administered fifteen to thirty minutes later, the memory is impaired. But if the shock is delayed for twenty-four hours, it has no effect on the memory. The theory now is that the first two stages of memory are electrical in nature, but that long-term memory takes a physical form in the brain much less evanescent than an electrical current.

The brain's electrochemical telegraph system

(See illustrations on pages 64-67)

At the center of the intelligence system in man and animals is the nerve cell or *neuron,* an extraordinary lacy structure, with many branching fibers and closely associated *glial* (i.e., sticky) cells. Some 10 billion neurons make up the brain and spinal cord in man, while millions more form the fine networks of the motor system, connecting brain to muscles, and the sensory system, connecting the brain to eyes, ears, nose, and other receptive links with the outer world. The neuron's main cell body holds the nucleus with its DNA-coded chromosomes, surrounded by the working parts and fluid of the cell. From it extends the main nerve fiber, or *axon,* for transmitting electrical nerve impulses, and shorter branched fibers or *dendrites* for receiving them. From the axon many twiglets branch off and make connections, called *synapses,* with other neurons. Each brain neuron makes hundreds of such synapses, and in turn receives hundreds from other neurons, so that a maze of extremely complex circuits is formed.

How the neuron generates and transmits electrical impulses is now known in some detail. There is a high concentration of potassium ions within the cell and a concentration of sodium ions outside. A negative electrical potential of some 70 millivolts across the cell membrane keeps sodium ions out, and prevents a current from flowing. When an impulse hits the neuron—from a sensory receptor, for example—it causes a breakdown of the potential voltage at the base of the axon, allowing sodium ions to flow in, and shooting a tiny electric current down the axon. Like the on-off switching components of a computer, the neuron either fires or does not fire, depending on whether the impulse it receives is strong enough to cross its threshold of response. The electric current courses down the axon in swift, complex stages, while sodium "gates" are closed behind it to prepare the cell for another incoming pulse; at each stage the ongoing pulse is somehow boosted to maintain its original force. Recently it has been found that this process is accompanied by a flow of fluid and cell particles down the axon, and that the surrounding glial cells contribute important ribonucleic acid (RNA) and energy-rich compounds to the action.

At the end of the axon, where it joins with another neuron, is a *synaptic knob*. This is separated by less than a millionth of an inch from the surface of the neuron and is connected only by filamentary threads. The tiny current in the axon cannot leap across this gap without further complex apparatus. This consists of small *synaptic vesicles* containing chemical transmitter substances, which are released when the impulse hits the synapse. The chemical transmitters drift across the gap, act upon the neuron by opening pores in its cell membrane to admit a quantity of sodium ions, and thus recreate an exact replica of the original nerve impulse. This process ensures the accurate modulation and control of nerve impulses. According to a new theory, this electrochemical system is controlled by a host of specific RNA, proteins, and transmitter substances, all of them made under the direction of the DNA of the nerve and glial cells. Thus DNA may ultimately act as the pattern maker of cognition, memory, and thought.

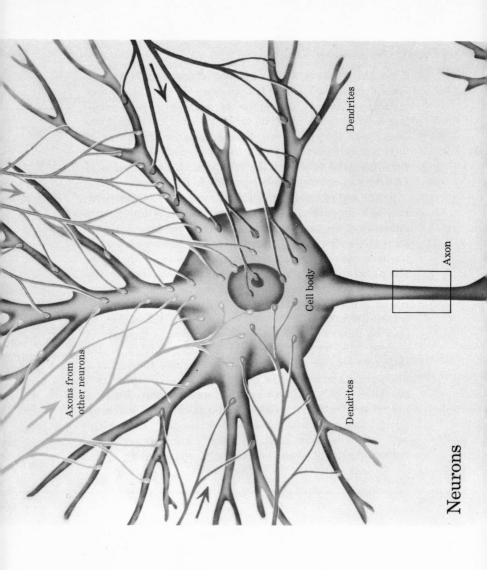

Neurons

Dendrites

Dendrites

Cell body

Axon

Axons from
other neurons

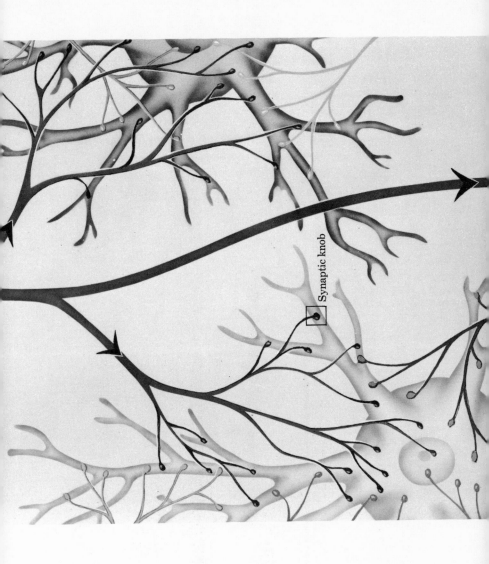

Synaptic knob

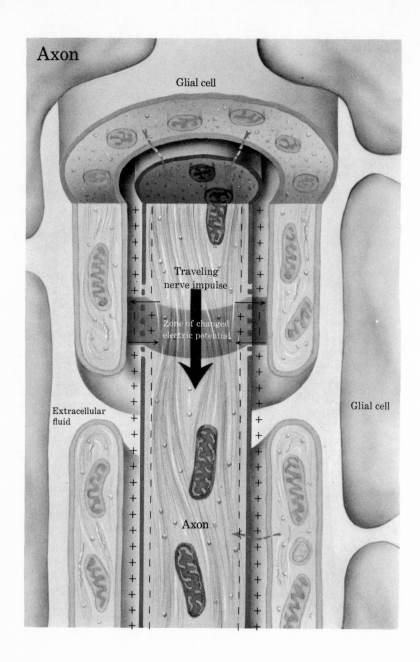

Axon

Glial cell

Glial cell

Traveling nerve impulse

Zone of changed electric potential

Extracellular fluid

Axon

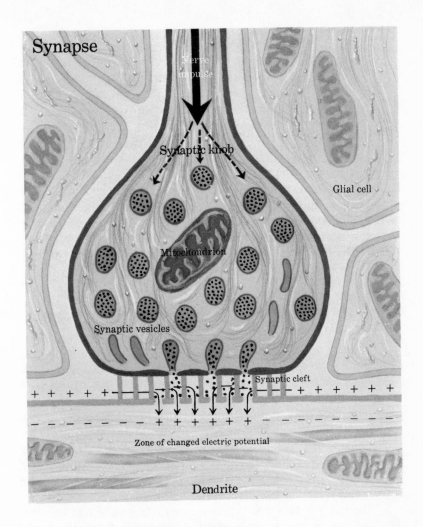

Synapse

Nerve impulse

Synaptic knob

Glial cell

Mitochondrion

Synaptic vesicles

Synaptic cleft

Zone of changed electric potential

Dendrite

Memory's permanent residence

A decade ago Wilder Penfield found what seemed to be a graphic demonstration of long-term memory. He was delicately probing with his fine electrodes into the cortex of patients undergoing brain operations. Under only local anesthetics, they remained conscious and able to speak. Suddenly his probe stimulated spots that instantly evoked from the patients a total recall, in vivid detail, of incidents that had happened many years before, often in childhood. It was as if, upon pressing a button, old cinematographic strips were run off in perfect sequence. Of course, the permanence of childhood memories is an imperishable part of all literature. But Penfield's patients remembered events in minute detail rarely encountered in books. Much of the recollection was so trivial that psychologists dispute whether it can be considered part of the conscious permanent memory at all.

Penfield went on to observe that this memory seemed to be localized in no particular area but was diffused over the whole cortex. This finding later received some substantiation in the famous split-brain experiments on cats and other vertebrates by Ronald E. Myers and others. These demonstrated that the two halves of the brain could operate separately at full capacity, indicating a great redundancy of memory and other elements. But if permanent memories are so widely dispersed in the brain, then in what physical entities do they reside?

A clue may come from a recent series of experiments by Roger W. Sperry of the California Institute of Technology. He has investigated the way in which growing nerve fibers find the right neurons on which to form synapses. In one experiment, he delicately cut the optic nerve fibers of goldfish, blinding them. In normal vision, the fish's optics are crossed: fibers from the left eye terminate in the brain's right lobe, fibers from the right eye in the left lobe, just as in man it is a well-known fact that all left-handed body functions are controlled in the right side of the brain and vice versa. When the goldfishes' optic fibers regenerated themselves—a feat possible only in lower vertebrates, amphibians, and fishes—their growing tips unerringly sought out and remade all the proper synaptic connections in the brain; i.e., the right eye's nerve fibers made synapses only with neurons in the left side of the brain. Not only that, but the new connections were all properly oriented according to their points of origin in the retinas of the eyes, so that the fishes' restored vision accurately distinguished up from down, left from right. The implication of this for human optics is that, in embryonic development, a million or so fibers from the eyes thus find precisely the right synaptic hookups in the brain. The only biological mechanism by which such precision could be attained, Sperry concludes, is a specific chemical or molecular identification between optic fibers and brain neurons.

This would account for the built-in precision of sensory systems and instinctive networks—what might be called the "permanent memory" of the species. But it does not yet account for the individual's later acquisitions of memory with time and experience, which must involve the making of whole new networks of synapses. It suggests, however, that this process, too, might well be specifically molecular or electrochemical in operation.

The "sticky-state" physics of the brain

To these tangled problems, molecular biology has brought an influx of new knowledge and powerful new tools and concepts. Obviously, such wired-in instinctual networks as the optic, motor, and emotional centers of the brain are direct products of the genetically coded DNA-RNA-protein factory of the cell and its differentiated development. It now seems equally obvious to many of the new biologists that, in more devious and elusive ways, specific molecules shaped by the DNA-RNA code must also act as the medium for carrying on all the higher brain functions of memory, learning, and even thought.

The first deep probing of this molecular level of the brain was made by a slim, cigar-smoking Swedish neurobiologist at the University of Göteborg, Holger Hydén. In order to get to the molecular level, he first had to perfect a technique to separate single live brain cells. The major trouble with brain chemistry in the past had been that it dealt with chunks of mixed tissues, and thus too often had got mixed and confusing results. Beginning about 1957, Hydén developed a set of fine stainless-steel tools, microknives, and minute wire hooks and prods with which to lift out single live neurons, smaller than a grain of dust. It took him a year of patient application to develop the freehand skills and routine procedures to do this under a stereomicroscope.

He then had to acquire more skills in order to "peel" off the smaller glial cells that cling like satellites to each neuron, and later to separate the neuron's cell body from its nucleus, so that each component could be analyzed separately for its RNA content, protein-enzyme activity, and other biologically active molecular ingredients. Thus he hoped to gain deep insight into the gelatinous electrical unit that makes the brain tick. Some whimsical biologists have dubbed this study "sticky-state" physics, in contrast to the solid-state physics of computers.

By 1960, Hydén and his colleagues at Göteborg had amassed a fund of startling experimental data. Rabbits, rats, and other test animals were run through experiments in which some were given merely ordinary sensory stimulation, such as being spun on a centrifuge, while others were taught new tasks, such as learning to climb a wire to get food. Immediately after a peak of such stimulation, they were killed and their individual neurons analyzed.

The scientists found that stimulation of any kind greatly raised the rate of RNA production, and hence protein synthesis, in the brain's neurons, which even normally are the richest of all body cells in RNA. Moreover, as the neuron's RNA activity increased, that of its associated glial cells declined, and vice versa. Thus it became evident that the glial cells, until then thought to be merely structural supports and insulators for neurons, are actively connected with the neuron system. When neuron activity is at its peak, the glia appear to supply RNA and energy-rich compounds to the neuron to sustain its excited firing of impulses; when the nerve quiets down the glia replenish their own store of RNA.

An information-retrieval system built on RNA

The most significant of Hydén's discoveries was that when the brain was stimulated experimentally by some form of learning exercise its RNA production not only increased, but a small fraction of this RNA differed in base sequence or chemical composition from any RNA found in the neurons of untrained control animals. The newly acquired learning seemed to be encoded in these different RNA molecules. Moreover, later refined experiments showed there was even a detectable difference in new RNA base sequences between the early stages of learning a task and late stages, suggesting that learning was actually being caught in the act of becoming fixed.

With these discoveries Hydén put the first physical footing under a provocative and still highly controversial molecular theory of memory and learning. It holds that, in the acquisition of new sensations or learning, modulated sensory impulses trigger in the neuron and its glial cells the production of specific RNA of a type not present in the cell before. These molecules of RNA store the memory of each impulse and are then available for its reevocation. At first the theory was misinterpreted in press reports, and even by some neurologists, to mean that the stored impulse is directly impressed or encoded on the RNA, as on an I.B.M. card; this would violate the genetic law that all molecular structures of an organism are controlled by the DNA code of its chromosomes and cannot acquire changed characteristics from the outside. Hydén believes that such a possibility cannot be entirely ruled out as yet, in the sense that incoming sensations may cause small additional changes in the structure of new RNA molecules thus produced. But the main burden of his theory, as he later clarified it, is that sensory impulses induce the activation in neural DNA of dormant genes, which then produce new RNA or RNA fractions to make the specific proteins or transmitter substances needed to "store" and reproduce the memory impulse.

There are some analogies in known biological systems to support this view. A similar theory of molecular information storage and retrieval is now believed to account for the immunological system by which the body's cells recognize a host of foreign invaders and then generate different protein antibodies specifically shaped to lock upon and overcome them. A group at the University of California, Berkeley, led by Mark Rosenzweig and David Krech, has broadly demonstrated in a long series of meticulous experiments on young rats that brains exposed to a stimulating learning environment are different in physical and cellular make-up from those which are not. The brain cortices of "learned" rats, after eighty days in the experiment, weighed 4.6 percent more on the average than those of their unstimulated litter mates, raised in isolation. Marked differences also occurred in the neurons' enzyme activity and other molecular constituents, and in an increase of glial cells. More specifically, other research experiments have recently suggested that retention of memory, learning, and other brain functions are dependent on RNA-protein synthesis. By injecting test animals with small amounts of puromycin, an antibiotic known to block RNA-mediated protein synthesis, the researchers effectively blocked the formation of lasting memory of newly learned tasks or recent events.

The worms that ate their education

The idea that memory might be contained in a molecule inspired a rather wild spate of experimentation. The most direct tests, some investigators reasoned, would be to transfer RNA molecules from the brains of trained animals into untrained ones, and observe results. James V. McConnell, an energetic young psychologist at the University of Michigan, chose planaria (common flatworms) as the simplest teachable animal to work with. In 1962 he made headlines with a report that his "educated" flatworms, taught to avoid an electroshock by contracting on a signal from a flashing light, had their learned responses transferred when they were chopped up and fed to untutored worms. The worms so fed learned to recognize the warning light about twice as fast as others not nourished on their educated brethren. Since then McConnell has extended his experiments to more intricate tasks.

In 1965 a group at U.C.L.A. under psychologist Allan Jacobson made an even bigger splash. They had worked up in the evolutionary scale to rats and hamsters, which were taught to take food from a box that opened at a signal from a flashing light or clicking sound. The U.C.L.A. experimenters reported that when RNA was extracted from the brains of these animals and injected into untrained ones, the neo-phytes showed "a significant tendency" to move toward the feedbox on signal. Moreover, this learning seemed to be trans-ferable from species to species—e.g., from rats to hamsters and vice versa.

All these results are now widely under dispute, however. Skeptics point out, for one thing, that the results of such be-havioral tests are notably tricky and often bent in the desired direction by the conditions of the experiment. For another, it seems highly unlikely that RNA, a rather delicate molecule, could get to the brain unscathed through the digestive sys-tem and the blood-brain barrier, a sac that keeps out large foreign and unwanted molecules. But the most telling argu-ment is that a number of other laboratories have tried to duplicate the McConnell and Jacobson experiments and have failed to get their results. As a consequence, the idea that memory or learning may be transferred from one individual to another in a molecule is under severe attack.

A more plausible research approach was simply to attempt to supplement or stimulate the brain's own general produc-tion of RNA. The first to try this, long before it was proposed that RNA had a specific role in memory, was D. Ewen Cam-eron, then head of McGill University's department of psy-chiatry. He gave doses of RNA extracted from yeast to groups of elderly human patients suffering loss of memory. He re-ported in 1958 and later that, if the memory loss had not gone too far, the patients showed some improvement in mem-ory retention, alertness, and mental attitude. But these re-sults met much the same objections as the animal transfer experiments, with the added drawback that tests on humans are much more prone to subjective interpretation.

A different tack was taken more recently by a research group associated with Abbott Laboratories in North Chicago. It set out to find a simple chemical compound that might get through to the brain and speed up the key enzyme-making

RNA there. In their search the Abbott investigators tested magnesium pemoline, long known in Europe as a mild general stimulant. Late last year they reported that this compound (tradenamed Cylert) showed a stimulating effect on the critical brain enzyme in test tubes and on isolated brain tissue; in behavioral tests on rats it speeded up learning and enhanced memory. The drug is being clinically tested on humans, by, among others, Cameron, now director of psychiatric and aging research at the Albany Veterans Administration Hospital. He reports some favorable preliminary results. But no one can say how the drug works, if indeed it works at all, and most authorities are extremely dubious, in the absence of more widespread objective tests, that a memory-enhancing drug has yet been found.

The whole field, in fact, is still in the early, groping stages of development. Most biologists doubt that the problem will be simply solved by finding a single "magic memory molecule." Some think memory is more likely to be traced in the complex biochemical system of molecules that modulate nerve impulses. Others think the key is to be found in the making of synapses, which would also be molecularly directed. It is perhaps predictable that the brain, so long resistant to understanding, will not yield readily to assault. But there is no doubt, even among disputing specialists, that molecular biologists are now on to something in the brain, and that in the steadily grinding course of research it will be run down.

100,000 brain cells lost every day

Science has gone far toward conquering many diseases and extending the average life span, but so far almost nothing has been found to slow or reverse the deterioration of the brain with age. Brain neurons, unlike most of the other body cells, do not divide or replenish themselves after development, and show only moderate growth through life. This is perhaps nature's way of preserving undisturbed the brain's information-storage system. The penalty, however, is that gradually neurons die and are not replaced. After a man reaches about thirty-five, on the average, he loses an estimated 100,000 neurons a day, and his memory slowly blurs into old age. The brain's glial cells, on the other hand, continue to reproduce at a slowing rate. So if a convenient compound could be found to stimulate the neurons' declining production of RNA or prod the glia into compensatory production, man's mental productivity could be extended well into old age. Biologists are hopeful of finding such agents. Some of them think it may even be possible someday, when more is known in detail about the brain's mechanisms, to learn how to encourage replacement of worn-out brain cells in a controlled way.

Growing knowledge of the brain's molecular mechanisms might also revolutionize the treatment of mental retardation, as well as nerve and mental diseases. At an excited medical symposium in New York early in 1964 four reports of different lines of research in Austrian, Canadian, and Swedish laboratories converged to show that Parkinson's disease, that muscle-disorganizing nerve malady, is definitely linked to a deficit of a chemical, dopamine, in the brain. Biochemists now have real hope of finding drugs or enzymes to compensate for this deficit. The deep-seated mental diseases, such as the various forms of schizophrenia, present a more difficult problem, which will probably require a much more comprehensive grasp of basic brain mechanisms than we now have. But the molecular principles and tools are rapidly coming to hand.

At the other, youthful end of the scale, the new knowledge foreshadows a great improvement in learning and educational processes, perhaps even improvement of the brain itself. A wide range of new experimental evidence, some of it from Hydén's group at the molecular level, shows that the brain requires both proper nutrition and stimulation to develop fully, especially in the early stages. Neurons deprived of either nutrition or stimulation—but particularly of a stimulating learning environment—fail to develop RNA-protein content, make no rich tangle of fiber connections, become more or less empty bags, and finally atrophy. The new research may spur large changes in the whole pace and schedule of education. Already, in such programs as Project Head Start, there is a movement to carry educational processes back even within the first year of birth. Psychologist David Krech estimates that such stimulating devices, plus motivation, might easily raise the general I.Q. level ten to twenty points, without the use of drugs or other aids. With the brain-enhancing drugs that seem certainly in store, the level might be raised spectacularly.

Conceivably, it may also be possible at the embryonic stage to develop bigger brains with a greater number of neurons, to accommodate the great expansion of modern knowledge. Undesirable characteristics, such as aggressive drives, might also be modified. And the suggestion has been made that one day man's brain may be provided with extrasensory equipment, such as microwave receiver and transmitter devices, to extend his range of communication and to put him in direct connection with his more and more sophisticated information-processing machines. "If man is not to become obsolete," says Caltech's James Bonner, "he must keep up in the development of his own brain power with the development of these machines which at present are our slaves."

Changing the course of evolution

The promises of benefits from such intervention in nature, however, must be hedged with warnings of abuse. The same techniques that may be used to turn off aggression in man could also be used to turn it on. The same types of memory-blocking compounds used to study the learning mechanism of the brain, which might be used medically to blot out shocking experiences, might also become useful tools for a police state. Other compounds have been found to make the brain more suggestible under instruction, and it is not beyond the realm of possibility that they could be used to condition whole groups and populations to servility. For the last three or four years biological meetings have been ringing with adjurations to take thought of consequences and set up safeguards.

Broadly speaking, the new biology holds forth the prospect of changing the course of human evolution, and by means that go far beyond those that used to be proposed by the eugenicists in their schemes for the planned breeding of humans for a more perfect society. Joshua Lederberg, the U.S. Nobel Prize-winning geneticist, who has been thoughtfully expounding on the subject, sees at least three ways in which molecular genetics could be employed to change human nature. The first approach, which he calls "algeny" or genetic alchemy, is to go directly to the germ cell or fertilized egg cell and alter individual genes by changing their DNA code to produce desired characteristics or to correct hereditary defects. The second route, "euphenics," is more indirect; it would involve modifying the functioning of the genes at the developmental stage or later by administering enzymes, hormones, or other chemical agents, such as brain-enhancing drugs, to make up deficiencies or to get entirely new effects. Lederberg believes euphenics is almost immediately applicable to medical practice and can have a much more rapid impact than algeny, which is more difficult and dangerous. Yet he believes that algeny, too, will eventually be achieved and used, perhaps sooner than many of his colleagues think.

But even closer to the experimental stage, according to Lederberg, is a third route to genetic change, which he calls somatic or body-cell genetics. It is based on the rapidly developing art of growing human tissue or body cells in cultures. Lederberg foresees two lines of development. One is to culture tissue lines in which the desired gene combinations are fixed, reset, or reordered, then grow from them whole organs (for transplants) or whole organisms. Since each body cell contains the full DNA code for the total organism, it should be possible to make an exact copy of a man by manipulating his tissue cells in a culture, then allowing one complete set of chromosomes to grow and develop within an egg cell. As Lederberg puts it, such an experiment would enable us "to discover whether a second Einstein would outdo the first one." As a second approach to body-cell development, Lederberg foresees the hybridization of cells from mixed human and animal sources, which is already being done in tissue cultures. From this line of development might grow various orders of subhuman or superhuman creatures, more fearsome and astounding than those of mythology.

Beyond the Hippocratic oath

As such hair-raising ideas move toward reality, they will raise ethical, moral, legal, and social issues unparalleled in history. Consider the socio-legal snarls that have already grown up around artificial insemination. How much knottier would be the questions posed by experimental alteration of the human embryo itself, or the laboratory creation of entirely new individuals. The current wrangling over control of the hallucinatory mind drug LSD is only symptomatic of the tangle of problems that will arise as science enlarges the repertoire of drugs acting specifically on the mind. If chemical techniques are developed for growing larger brains, should they be available to the few or the many? And what of the liability, attendant upon all mind-reaching drugs, of effecting unforeseen or undesirable shifts or changes in the human personality?

The whole touchy issue of medical experimentation on human beings reaches a new pitch of sensitivity in the area of molecular genetics and biology. Common law and judicial decision provide some legal redress for medical mistakes. But the law and its interpretation are essentially vague and hardly cover many of the real situations now opening up under biological advances. The physician's Hippocratic oath protects the individual from willful experiment, but it, too, barely covers some of the newer developments. Obviously some new form of regulation is required in certain areas. But should regulation go to the extent of interdicting all basic research in these new biological areas? This would at once cut off beneficial advances. In the end, the prohibition would prove impossible to enforce, since all basic discoveries, such as the shape and code of DNA itself, start out as mental concepts, which no man or state can prevent men from conceiving.

When all is said and done, there is no firmer basis for meeting the new challenges than to ensure the widest dispersal of the new knowledge, so that men may begin to understand its implications and develop a community consensus on how to go about using it. Humanity is embarked on still another uncharted course, as fateful as the splitting of the atom, as prodigious as the exploration of outer space.

Index

Abbott Laboratories, 74-75
Acetylcholine, 59
Acids
  amino, 17, 22
    coding problem of, 16-18
  nucleic, 17
  See also Deoxyribonucleic acid
    (DNA) and Ribonucleic acid
    (RNA)
Adenine (A), 2-3, 9, 15
Adrenal hormones, 47-48
Agammaglobulinemia, 22
Albinos, 22
Algeny, 78
Allfrey, Vincent G., 40
Alpha rhythm, the, 58

American Association for the Advancement of Science, 56
Amino acid, 17, 22
  coding problem of, 16-18
Anemia, sickle-cell, 22
Antibodies, 48-50, 72
  composition of, 49-50
Australian National University, 59
Avco Corporation, 25
Avery, Oswald T., 13, 24
Axon, the, 62-63

Bacteria, virulent, 7-13
Beadle, George W., 19, 24-25
Bennett, J. Claude, 49
Berger, Hans, 58